7/2/1[?]

To the M[?]
Beautiful Mom,
      My mom

I hope you
enjoy this book—
I know you
always liked
the footprints!
I do remember

                Love
                Lily

A Gift for :

_____

From:

_____

May the God of hope fill you
with all joy and peace as you trust in him,
so that you may overflow with hope
by the power of the Holy Spirit.

§

ROMANS 15:13

FOOTPRINTS

One night I dreamed a dream.
I was walking along the beach with my Lord.
Across the dark sky flashed scenes from my life.
For each scene, I noticed two sets of footprints in
 the sand,
one belonging to me
and one to my Lord.
When the last scene of my life shot before me
I looked back at the footprints in the sand
and to my surprise
I noticed that many times along the path of my life
There was only one set of footprints.
I realized that this was at the lowest
and saddest times of my life.
This always bothered me
and I questioned the Lord
about my dilemma.
"Lord, you told me when I decided to follow You,
You would walk and talk with me all the way.
But I'm aware that during the most troublesome
times of my life there is only one set of footprints.
I just don't understand why, when I needed You
 most, You leave me."
He whispered, "My precious child,
I love you and will never leave you
never, ever, during your trials and testings.
When you saw only one set of footprints
it was then that I carried you."

© 1964 Margaret Fishback Powers

footprints

SCRIPTURE WITH REFLECTIONS

INSPIRED BY THE BEST-LOVED POEM

BY MARGARET FISHBACK POWERS

inspirio™

GIFT BOOKS
from Hallmark

BOK3085

Footprints: Scripture with Reflections Inspired by the Best-Loved Poem
by Margaret Fishback Powers
Copyright © 1998 by Margaret Fishback Powers
ISBN 10: 1-59530-142-9
ISBN 13: 978-1-59530-142-0

Published in 2006 under license from Zondervan Publishing
House exclusively for Hallmark Cards, Inc.
Visit us on the Web at www.Hallmark.com.

Excerpts taken from: *The Footprints Book of Prayers.* Copyright ©
1996 by Margaret Fishback Powers; *Life's Little Inspiration Book II.*
Copyright © 1995 by Margaret Fishback Powers. *Footprints.*
Copyright © 1996 by Margaret Fishback Powers.

Associate Publisher: Tom Dean
Design Manager: Val Buick
Designer: Gayle Raymer

Printed in China

09 10 11 / TSC / 13 12 11 10

INTRODUCTION

*E*very now and then during our devotional time, my husband, Paul, and I reread the poem I wrote for him back in 1964. During these times of renewal and prayer, we talk over the events of our lives and share burdens we have for ourselves and others. Very often, we realize that the Great Shepherd has once again reached out and carried us through the day as we spend these introspective moments together.

If the pleasure of sharing these thoughts anew has taught us anything, it is this: that God's Word is true. Our heavenly Father is faithful and will never leave us or forsake us. As we come to him daily, willing to be shaped and directed, his Word gives guideposts of clear direction. Almost everything we read, see, and experience shows us in some way that, although we do not visibly see God, he is with us. Over centuries of time, others have looked back to understand that God's Spirit and presence were there, even when they felt alone.

In our quiet moments of reflection, in the fellowship of others, and even in dreams, God opens the doors to our hearts. This is what happened when I originally wrote the poem "Footprints."

After hours of wrestling with the darkness of doubt and despair, I finally surrendered to him and, in the early-morning light of peace, wrote the poem as result of that spiritual experience.

Listen for the gentle stirring of God's grace in your own mind and soul as you read these verses of encouragement. Reflecting on his Word will help you to know him better.

Spiritual growth is not so much what we have done, but the feeling of love for him we put into everything we do. It is not so much in knowing about God that we grow, but in getting to *know him* in a personal, relational way. It is in becoming "a friend of God" as Abraham did that we grow in his grace, talking with him as our companion along the way, and letting God sift our thoughts and plans through the standards of his Word. May these verses encourage you anew each day as you walk with him.

MARGARET FISHBACK POWERS

In Our Dreams

One night I dreamed a dream.

Some of our dreams can have a powerful effect on us. All of us have, at one time or another, awakened laughing or fretful—and all because of a dream. The Bible tells us about many people who had dreams and visions that were given to them by God ...

[Jacob] had a dream in which he saw a stairway resting on the earth, with its top reaching to heaven, and the angels of God were ascending and descending on it.

GENESIS 28:12

Joseph had a dream, and when he told it to his brothers, they hated him all the more.

GENESIS 37:5

At Gibeon the LORD appeared to Solomon during the night in a dream, and God said, "Ask for whatever you want me to give you."

1 KINGS 3:5

An angel of the Lord appeared to Joseph in a dream. "Get up," he said, "take the child and his mother and escape to Egypt. Stay there until I tell you, for Herod is going to search for the child to kill him."

MATTHEW 2:13

After Herod died, an angel of the Lord appeared in a dream to Joseph in Egypt and said, "Get up, take the child and his mother and go to the land of Israel, for those who were trying to take the child's life are dead."

MATTHEW 2:19–20

One day at about three in the afternoon
[Cornelius] had a vision. He distinctly saw an
angel of God, who came to him and said,
"Cornelius!"

ACTS 10:3

During the night Paul had a vision of a man
of Macedonia standing and begging him,
"Come over to Macedonia and help us."

ACTS 16:9

Some of our dreams are disappointing, but
these are "wishful-thinking" dreams, things we
come up with in our own minds, circumstances
or situations that we wish would happen. Only
a small portion of these kinds of dreams ever
come true. In fact, these dreams can be harm-
ful if we allow them to fill us with false hope…

This is what the LORD Almighty says:
"Do not listen to what the
         prophets are prophesying
         to you;
     they fill you with false hopes.
They speak visions from their
         own minds,
         not from the mouth of the
         LORD."

JEREMIAH 23:16

$\mathcal{Y}$et we should not ignore our dreams. God will sometimes use our dreams to assure us of his promises or to tell us something about himself. And when God does speak to us in dreams, he will also help us understand them...

> [God] said, "Listen to my words:
>> "When a prophet of the LORD is
>>> among you,
>> I reveal myself to him in
>>> visions,
>> I speak to him in dreams."
>>>> NUMBERS 12:6

> [The LORD says,] I will pour out my Spirit on
>> all people.
> Your sons and daughters will
>> prophesy,
>> your old men will dream
>>> dreams,
>> your young men will see
>>> visions.
>>>> JOEL 2:28

$\mathcal{G}$od's presence with us is a reality. Acts 2:17 also tells us that God will pour his "Spirit on all people." As we dream our dreams with the knowledge that God is with us, we will begin to see things as Christ does and dream dreams inspired by the Holy Spirit that are worth re-telling and following.

In Our Daily Walk

*I was walking along the
beach with my Lord.*

A close walk with the Lord is an important part of a believer's life...

> *[God] will teach us his ways,*
>   *so that we may walk in his*
>   *paths.*
>
> ISAIAH 2:3

May [God] turn our hearts to him, to walk in all his ways and to keep the commands, decrees and regulations he gave our fathers.

1 KINGS 8:58

> *Your love is ever before me, [LORD,]*
>   *and I walk continually in*
>   *your truth.*
>
> PSALM 26:3

> *Walk in the way of*
>   *understanding.*
>
> PROVERBS 9:6

> *He whose walk is upright*
>   *fears the LORD.*
>
> PROVERBS 14:2

> *The ways of the LORD are*
>   *right;*
>   *the righteous walk in them.*
>
> HOSEA 14:9

> *He whose walk is blameless is*
>   *kept safe.*
>
> PROVERBS 28:18

Let us walk in the light of
*the L*ORD*.*

ISAIAH 2:5

Whether you turn to the right or to the left,
your ears will hear a voice behind you, saying,
"This is the way; walk in it."

ISAIAH 30:21

The Bible tells us that maintaining a close
walk with God is a command we must obey, not
merely a suggestion we may want to consider.

I am God Almighty; walk before me and be
blameless.

GENESIS 17:1

What does the LORD your God ask of you but
to fear the LORD your God, to walk in all his
ways, to love him, to serve the LORD your God
with all your heart and with all your soul.

DEUTERONOMY 10:12

Love the LORD your God...walk in all his
ways...hold fast to him.

DEUTERONOMY 11:22

The LORD will establish you...if you keep the
commands of the LORD your God and walk in
his ways.

DEUTERONOMY 28:9

[God] has showed you, O man,
what is good.
And what does the Lord
require of you?
To act justly and to love
mercy
and to walk humbly with
your God.

MICAH 6:8

This is love: that we walk in obedience to [God's] commands. As you have heard from the beginning, his command is that you walk in love.

2 JOHN 6

Obey me, and I will be your God and you will be my people. Walk in all the ways I command you, that it may go well with you.

JEREMIAH 7:23

Be very careful to keep the commandment and the law that Moses the servant of the Lord gave you: to love the Lord your God, to walk in all his ways, to obey his commands, to hold fast to him and to serve him with all your heart and all your soul.

JOSHUA 22:5

$\mathcal{B}$ut what does a walk with God actually entail? How does God want us to live?

> Love the LORD your God with all your heart and with all your soul and with all your strength. These commandments that I give you today are to be upon your hearts. Impress them on your children. Talk about them when you sit at home and when you walk along the road, when you lie down and when you get up.
>
> DEUTERONOMY 6:5–7

He whose walk is blameless
*   and who does what is*
*   righteous,*
who speaks the truth from his
*   heart*
*   and has no slander on his*
*   tongue,*
who does his neighbor no
*   wrong*
*   and casts no slur on his*
*   fellowman,*
who despises a vile man
*   but honors those who fear*
*   the LORD,*
who keeps his oath
*   even when it hurts,*
who lends his money without
*   usury*
*   and does not accept a bribe*
*   against the innocent.*
He who does these things
*   will never be shaken.*

PSALM 15:2–5

15

*M*any of these things that God asks us to do go against our nature. Yet Nehemiah asks us, "Shouldn't you walk in the fear of our God to avoid...reproach?" (Nehemiah 5:9). The Bible urges us to consistently walk with the Lord, walking by faith, even when it's difficult.

Live a life worthy of the Lord...please him in every way: bearing fruit in every good work, growing in the knowledge of God.
COLOSSIANS 1:10

Just as you received Christ Jesus as Lord, continue to live in him.
COLOSSIANS 2:6

If we walk in the light, as he is in the light, we have fellowship with one another, and the blood of Jesus, his Son, purifies us from all sin.
1 JOHN 1:7

Whoever claims to live in [God] must walk as Jesus did.
1 JOHN 2:6

We live by faith, not by sight.
2 CORINTHIANS 5:7

[Jesus said,] "Walk while you have the light, before darkness overtakes you. The man who walks in the dark does not know where he is going. Put your trust in the light while you have it, so that you may become sons of light."

JOHN 12:35–36

Live a life of love, just as Christ loved us.

EPHESIANS 5:2

*H*ealth professionals suggest that people who want to become physically fit should try a consistent program of walking. Sustained walking several times a week will improve your muscle tone and strengthen your heart.

The Bible reassures us that our spiritual lives will also reap benefits when we are consistent in walking with the Lord. Look at the many benefits a walk with God provides ...

Walk in all the way that the LORD your God has commanded you, so that you may live and prosper and prolong your days in the land that you will possess.

DEUTERONOMY 5:33

I will walk among you and be your God, and you will be my people.

LEVITICUS 26:12

I command you today to love the LORD your God, to walk in his ways, and to keep his commands, decrees and laws; then you will live and increase, and the LORD your God will bless you.

DEUTERONOMY 30:16

Observe what the LORD your God requires: Walk in his ways...so that you may prosper in all you do and wherever you go.

1 KINGS 2:3

Blessed are they whose ways
        are blameless,
    who walk according to the
        law of the LORD.
Blessed are they who keep his
        statutes
    and seek him with all their
        heart.
They do nothing wrong;
    they walk in his ways.

PSALM 119:1–3

[God said,] "If you walk in my ways and obey my statutes and commands...I will give you a long life."

1 KINGS 3:14

[The LORD says,] "If you do whatever I command you and walk in my ways and do what is right in my eyes by keeping my statutes and commands...I will be with you."

1 KINGS 11:38

*Blessed are all who fear the
      LORD,
   who walk in his ways.
You will eat the fruit of your
      labor;
   blessings and prosperity
   will be yours.*

PSALM 128:1-2

*I guide you in the way of
      wisdom
   and lead you along straight
      paths.
When you walk, your steps will
      not be hampered;
   when you run, you will not
      stumble.*

PROVERBS 4:11-12

*The LORD God is a sun and
      shield;
   the LORD bestows favor and
      honor;
no good thing does he
      withhold
   from those whose walk is
      blameless.*

PSALM 84:11

[The LORD says,] "Obey me, and I will be
your God and you will be my people. Walk in
all the ways I command you, that it may go
well with you."

JEREMIAH 7:23

We are the temple of the living God. As God has said: "I will live with them and walk among them, and I will be their God, and they will be my people."

2 CORINTHIANS 6:16

This is what the LORD says:
"Stand at the crossroads and
*   look;*
*   ask for the ancient paths,*
ask where the good way is,
*   and walk in it,*
*   and you will find rest for*
*   your souls."*

JEREMIAH 6:16

𝓕anny Crosby once said that the Lord "lovingly guards my footsteps and gives me songs in the night." A joyful heart is the mark of one who has a consistent walk with the Lord, who follows in the footsteps of the Master.

Take strength then, and be blessed in a close walk with the Lord, for "I will strengthen them in the LORD and in his name they will walk," declares the LORD (Zechariah 10:12).

In the Hard Times

Across the dark sky
flashed scenes from my life.

We all go through times when life seems to overwhelm us. The Bible reassures us that God's presence is with us to help us, even when we don't realize it.

> God is our refuge and
>   strength,
>   an ever-present help in
>   trouble.
>
> PSALM 46:1

> In my distress I called to the
>   LORD,
>   and he answered me...
> I called for help,
>   and you listened to my cry.
>
> JONAH 2:2

> Those who know your name
>   will trust in you,
>   for you, LORD, have never
>   forsaken those who
>   seek you.
>
> PSALM 9:10

> You are my hiding place;
>   you will protect me from
>   trouble
>   and surround me with songs
>   of deliverance.
>
> PSALM 32:7

My soul finds rest in God
            alone;
       my salvation comes from
            him.
He alone is my rock and my
            salvation;
       he is my fortress, I will never
            be shaken.

                    PSALM 62:1—2

Praise be to the Lord, to God
            our Savior,
       who daily bears our
            burdens.

                    PSALM 68:19

*M*oments of darkness in our lives may be caused by the death of a loved one, the loss of a job or a home, or another great tragedy of life. Yet there is a greater darkness than these tragedies: the darkness in the eyes of one who has not felt God's love, grace, and the assurance of his hope. There is hope for all of us. There is light. Jesus Christ, the Son of God, is our hope and light in the darkness.

> For you were once darkness, but now you are light in the LORD. Live as children of light.
>
>   EPHESIANS 5:8

Let him who walks in the dark,
  who has no light,
trust in the name of the LORD
  and rely on his God.

The people walking in darkness
  have seen a great light;
on those living in the land of
    the shadow of death
  a light has dawned.

ISAIAH 9:2

[Jesus] said, "I am the light of the world. Whoever follows me will never walk in darkness, but will have the light of life."

JOHN 8:12

[Jesus said,] "I have come into the world as a light, so that no one who believes in me should stay in darkness."

JOHN 12:46

Darkness covers the earth
and thick darkness is over
the peoples,
but the LORD rises upon you
and his glory appears over
you.

The LORD will be your
everlasting light,
and your God will be your
glory.

ISAIAH 60:19

Though I have fallen, I will
rise.
Though I sit in darkness,
the LORD will be my light...
He will bring me out into the
light;
I will see his righteousness.

MICAH 7:8—9

Because of the tender mercy of our God...
the rising sun will come to us from heaven
to shine on those living in darkness
and in the shadow of death,
to guide our feet into the path of peace.

LUKE 1:78—79

Our dark times may also be times when God wants to teach us something more about ourselves and his love for us. Our faith can be strengthened if we will wait patiently and trust God's heart-desire to make us more like himself.

> *A righteous man may have*
> *   many troubles,*
> * but the LORD delivers him*
> *   from them all.*
>   PSALM 34:19

> *Though you have made me see*
> *   troubles, many and*
> *   bitter,*
> * you will restore my life*
> *   again;*
> *from the depths of the earth*
> * you will again bring me up.*
>   PSALM 71:20

We must go through many hardships to enter the kingdom of God.
                          ACTS 14:22

Our light and momentary troubles are achieving for us an eternal glory that far outweighs them all. So we fix our eyes not on what is seen, but on what is unseen. For what is seen is temporary, but what is unseen is eternal.

    2 CORINTHIANS 4:17–18

Be joyful in hope, patient in affliction, faithful in prayer.

ROMANS 12:12

Do not be surprised at the painful trial you
are suffering, as though something strange
were happening to you. But rejoice that you
participate in the sufferings of Christ, so that
you may be overjoyed when his glory is
revealed.

1 PETER 4:12–13

*T*ragedy or testing, dark days or dreary nights,
God knows what we are facing. He is in touch
with what is happening to us, and he is concerned.

His eyes are on the ways of
men;
he sees their every step.

JOB 34:21

[Jesus said,] "I have told you these things, so
that in me you may have peace. In this world
you will have trouble. But take heart! I have
overcome the world."

JOHN 16:33

Though I walk in the midst
of trouble,
you preserve my
life…
with your right hand you
save me.

PSALM 138:7

He knows the way that I
*   take;*
*   when he has tested me, I*
*   will come forth as gold.*

JOB 23:10

I will be glad and rejoice in
*   your love,*
*   for you saw my affliction*
*   and knew the anguish of*
*   my soul.*

PSALM 31:7

When you pass through the
*   waters,*
*   I will be with you;*
and when you pass through the
*   rivers,*
*   they will not sweep over you.*
When you walk through the
*   fire,*
*   you will not be burned;*
*   the flames will not set you*
*   ablaze.*

ISAIAH 43:2

GOD IS WITH US...

As Our Companion

*For each scene, I noticed
two sets of footprints in
the sand, one belonging to me
and one to my Lord.*

I have a friend who loves to take long walks with me. We talk and laugh and enjoy each other's company as we stroll along. The exercise is beneficial, and so is the conversation.

The Lord is a lot like my friend. He enjoys walking with us as our companion on life's pathway. And he brings blessing into our lives when we walk closely with him.

> If we walk in the light, as he is in the light, we have fellowship with one another, and the blood of Jesus, his Son, purifies us from all sin.
>
> 1 JOHN 1:7

> Walk in [God's] ways, and keep his decrees and commands, his laws and requirements... so that you may prosper in all you do and wherever you go.
>
> 1 KINGS 2:3

> *Blessed are those who have*
> *learned to acclaim you,*
> *who walk in the light of*
> *your presence, O LORD.*
>
> PSALM 89:15

> Walk in all the way that the LORD your God has commanded you, so that you may live and prosper and prolong your days in the land that you will possess.
>
> DEUTERONOMY 5:33

> I will walk among you and be your God, and you will be my people.
>
> LEVITICUS 26:12

"If you walk in my ways and obey my statutes and commands...I will give you a long life," [says the LORD.]

1 KINGS 3:14

Blessed are all who fear the
*   LORD,*
*   who walk in his ways.*
You will eat the fruit of your
*   labor;*
*   blessings and prosperity*
*   will be yours.*

PSALM 128:1–2

Come...
*   let us walk in the light of*
*   the LORD.*

ISAIAH 2:5

We are the temple of the living God. As God has said: "I will live with them and walk among them, and I will be their God, and they will be my people."

2 CORINTHIANS 6:16

[The LORD said,] "If you do whatever I command you and walk in my ways and do what is right in my eyes by keeping my statutes and commands...I will be with you."

1 KINGS 11:38

Ask where the good way is,
*   and walk in it,*
*   and you will find rest for*
*   your souls.*

JEREMIAH 6:16

Though I walk in the midst
of trouble,
you preserve my
life;
you stretch out your hand...
with your right hand you
save me.

The awareness of God's presence with us is encouraging and heartwarming. It is as if we were two friends seated beside a rippling brook, enjoying a gentle breeze on a warm spring afternoon.

"Here I am! I stand at the door and knock. If anyone hears my voice and opens the door, I will come in and eat with him, and he with me," says the Lord.

REVELATION 3:20

Come near to God and he will come near to you.

JAMES 4:8

"Abraham believed God, and it was credited to him as righteousness," and he was called God's friend.

JAMES 2:23

I am a friend to all who fear
you,
to all who follow your
precepts.

PSALM 119:63

[Jesus said,] "You are my friends if you do what I command....I have called you friends, for everything that I learned from my Father I have made known to you. You did not choose me, but I chose you."

JOHN 15:14–16

*E*ven when we are surrounded by family and friends, some problems seem to double in size of their own accord. If we toss and turn in the early morning hours thinking about them, they become ten times as large. Yet, although it may seem the whole world has gone wrong around us, we are not alone—God is with us!

So do not fear, for I am with
you;
do not be dismayed, for I am
your God.
I will strengthen you and help
you;
I will uphold you with my
righteous right hand.

ISAIAH 41:10

[Jesus said,] "I will not leave you as orphans; I will come to you."

JOHN 14:18

"For where two or three come together in my name, there am I with them," [Jesus said.]

MATTHEW 18:20

Who shall separate us from the love of Christ?
Shall trouble or hardship or persecution or
famine or nakedness or danger or sword?...
No, in all these things we are more than conquerors through him who loved us. For I am
convinced that neither death nor life, neither
angels nor demons, neither the present nor
the future, nor any powers, neither height nor
depth, nor anything else in all creation, will
be able to separate us from the love of God
that is in Christ Jesus our Lord.

ROMANS 8:35–39

For the LORD your God is a merciful God; he
will not abandon or destroy you or forget the
covenant with your forefathers, which he
confirmed to them by oath.

DEUTERONOMY 4:31

God is our refuge and
strength,
an ever-present help in
trouble.

PSALM 46:1

"Though the mountains be
shaken
and the hills be removed,
yet my unfailing love for you
will not be shaken
nor my covenant of peace
be removed,"
says the LORD, who has
compassion on you.

ISAIAH 54:10

"He will call upon me, and I will
answer him;
I will be with him in trouble,
I will deliver him and honor
him.
With long life will I satisfy
him
and show him my
salvation," [says the LORD.]

P SALM   9 1 : 1 5 — 1 6

[LORD,] where can I go from your
Spirit?
Where can I flee from your
presence?
If I go up to the heavens, you
are there;
if I make my bed in the
depths, you are there.
If I rise on the wings of the
dawn,
if I settle on the far side of
the sea,
even there your hand will guide
me,
your right hand will hold me
fast.

P SALM   1 3 9 : 7 — 1 0

Wherever we go, we cannot step outside the boundaries of God's love and care. We can have fellowship "with the Father and with his Son, Jesus Christ" wherever we are (1 John 1:3). All we need to do is trust in God's loving companionship and walk the path he has placed before us.

> *He will not let your foot slip—*
>   *he who watches over you will*
>   *not slumber.*
> *The LORD watches over you—*
>   *the LORD is your shade at*
>   *your right hand;*
> *the sun will not harm you by*
>   *day,*
>   *nor the moon by night.*
> *The LORD will keep you from all*
>   *harm—*
>   *he will watch over your life;*
> *the LORD will watch over your*
>   *coming and going*
>   *both now and forevermore.*
>   PSALM 121:3, 5—8

[Then Jesus said,] "And surely I am with you always, to the very end of the age."
    MATTHEW 28:20

GOD IS WITH US...

Never Look Back!
No Regrets!

When the last scene of my life
shot before me, I looked back
at the footprints in the sand.

We say that hindsight is always 20/20. Looking back is something we often do without considering the consequences. However, looking back is not recommended in the Bible. Lot was warned not to look back toward Sodom and Gomorrah...

> With the coming of dawn, the angels urged Lot, saying..."Flee for your lives! Don't look back, and don't stop anywhere in the plain! Flee to the mountains or you will be swept away!" Then the LORD rained down burning sulfur on Sodom and Gomorrah...Thus he overthrew those cities and the entire plain... But Lot's wife looked back, and she became a pillar of salt.
>
> GENESIS 19:15, 17, 24—26

Joshua and his men attacked their enemies in the city of Ai and quickly set the city on fire. When the men of Ai looked back, disaster fell on them...

> The men of Ai looked back and saw the smoke of the city rising against the sky, but they had no chance to escape in any direction, for the Israelites who had been fleeing toward the desert had turned back against their pursuers.
>
> JOSHUA 8:20

*E*ven the Lord Jesus reminded his listeners of the perils of looking back...

> Jesus replied, "No one who puts his hand to the plow and looks back is fit for service in the kingdom of God."
>
> LUKE 9:62

*W*hen we live with an attitude that looks back over our lives with "if onlys and regrets, we rob ourselves of hope. We rob ourselves of the joy of God's grace.

> ["God] has delivered us from such a deadly peril, and he will deliver us. On him we have set our hope that he will continue to deliver us."
>
> 2 CORINTHIANS 1:10

> I do not consider myself yet to have taken hold of it. But one thing I do: Forgetting what is behind and straining toward what is ahead, I press on toward the goal to win the prize for which God has called me heaven-ward in Christ Jesus.
>
> PHILIPPIANS 3:13–14

God never changes. He is the God of grace. He is the God of hope. He is the God of love who offers us a life free of regrets.

> God is greater than our hearts, and he knows everything.
>
> 1 JOHN 3:20

> *From everlasting to*
> *everlasting*
> *the LORD's love is with those*
> *who fear him,*
> *and his righteousness with*
> *their children's*
> *children—*
> *with those who keep his*
> *covenant*
> *and remember to obey his*
> *precepts.*
>
> PSALM 103:17–18

A life without regrets does not mean a life without repentance. When we sin, we must go beyond regretting and feeling sorry for our actions. We must move on to repentance by turning from our sinful ways and embracing God's forgiveness.

> Godly sorrow brings repentance that leads to salvation and leaves no regret.
>
> 2 CORINTHIANS 7:10

Cleanse me with hyssop, and
I will be clean;
wash me, and I will be whiter
than snow....
Hide your face from my sins
and blot out all my iniquity.
Create in me a pure heart,
O God,
and renew a steadfast spirit
within me.
Do not cast me from your
presence
or take your Holy Spirit
from me.
Restore to me the joy of your
salvation
and grant me a willing spirit,
to sustain me.

PSALM 51:7−12

(*W*)hen we have experienced God's forgiveness, we are new creatures. We do not need to live a life of regrets, but rather we can live with a forward-looking hope of glory!

> Let us throw off everything that hinders and the sin that so easily entangles, and let us run with perseverance the race marked out for us. Let us fix our eyes on Jesus, the author and perfecter of our faith.

HEBREWS 12:1−2

> If anyone is in Christ, he is a new creation; the old has gone, the new has come!

2 CORINTHIANS 5:17

I have fought the good fight, I have finished the race, I have kept the faith. Now there is in store for me the crown of righteousness, which the Lord, the righteous Judge, will award to me on that day.

2 TIMOTHY 4:7–8

Whenever we do look back over our lives, we must do so with God's perspective—no remorse or regrets. With God's perspective, we will be able to trace his hand on our lives and see that he has swept up the bad things of life and transformed them into good, just as he promised he would. With God's perspective, we will be able to live above regrets and live in God's peace and joy.

We know that in all things God works for the good of those who love him, who have been called according to his purpose.

ROMANS 8:28

Surely goodness and love will
follow me
all the days of my life,
and I will dwell in the house of
the LORD
forever.

PSALM 23:6

GOD IS WITH US...

In Our Loneliness

There was only one
set of footprints.

*T*oddlers often face separation anxiety—a feeling of abandonment whenever their parents leave the room. Though we may be much older and wiser than little children, we still feel the pain of loneliness and isolation. Both Jesus and the psalmist also knew what it was to feel alone, abandoned, forgotten ...

About the ninth hour Jesus cried out in a loud voice, *"Eloi, Eloi, lama sabachthani?"*— which means, "My God, my God, why have you forsaken me?"

M A T T H E W 2 7 : 4 6

Do not hide your face from
*   me,*
*   do not turn your servant*
*   away in anger;*
*   you have been my helper.*
Do not reject me or forsake me,
*   O God my Savior.*

P S A L M 2 7 : 9

I say to God my Rock,
*   "Why have you forgotten me?*
Why must I go about
*   mourning,*
*   oppressed by the enemy?"*

P S A L M 4 2 : 9

When we feel alone and abandoned we can take comfort in God's promises to deliver us from our isolation and pain.

> Can a mother forget the baby
>   at her breast
>   and have no compassion on
>   the child she has borne?
> Though she may forget,
>   I will not forget you!
> See, I have engraved you on
>   the palms of my hands.
>
> ISAIAH 49:15—16

> I the LORD will answer
>   them;
>   I, the God of Israel, will not
>   forsake them.
>
> ISAIAH 41:17

> You are enthroned as the
>   Holy One;
>   you are the praise of
>   Israel.
> In you our fathers put their
>   trust;
>   they trusted and you
>   delivered them.
> They cried to you and were
>   saved;
>   in you they trusted and were
>   not disappointed.
>
> PSALM 22:3—5

The LORD will not reject his people, because the LORD was pleased to make you his own.

1 SAMUEL 12:22

[Jesus said,] "I will not leave you as orphans; I will come to you."

JOHN 14:18

God is our refuge and
strength,
an ever-present help in
trouble.

PSALM 46:1

The eternal God is your refuge, and underneath are the everlasting arms.

DEUTERONOMY 33:27

"Though the mountains be
shaken
and the hills be removed,
yet my unfailing love for you
will not be shaken
nor my covenant of peace
be removed,"
says the LORD.

ISAIAH 54:10

"Do not let your hearts be troubled. Trust in God; trust also in me," [Jesus said.]

JOHN 14:1

How great is your goodness, [O LORD,]
which you have stored up for
those who fear you,
which you bestow in the sight
of men
on those who take refuge in
you.
In the shelter of your presence
you hide them...
in your dwelling you keep them
safe.

PSALM 31:19–20

He will not let your foot slip—
he who watches over you will
not slumber.
The LORD watches over you—
the LORD is your shade at
your right hand;
the sun will not harm you by
day,
nor the moon by night.
The LORD will keep you from all
harm—
he will watch over your life;
the LORD will watch over your
coming and going
both now and forevermore.

PSALM 121:3, 5–8

God is always with us—in our joy and in our pain, in the good times and in the bad times. His steadfast love and faithfulness are promises to which we can cling, promises to bring us joy when we face loneliness.

[And Jesus told his disciples,] "And surely I am with you always, to the very end of the age."

MATTHEW 28:20

The LORD your God is a merciful God; he will not abandon or destroy you.

DEUTERONOMY 4:31

Be strong and courageous. Do not be afraid or terrified…for the LORD your God goes with you; he will never leave you nor forsake you.

DEUTERONOMY 31:6

"Here I am! I stand at the door and knock. If anyone hears my voice and opens the door, I will come in and eat with him, and he with me," [says the LORD.]

REVELATION 3:20

You have made him glad with the joy of your presence.

PSALM 21:6

Those who know your name will trust in you, for you, LORD, have never forsaken those who seek you.

PSALM 9:10

[O LORD,] Where can I go from your
       Spirit?
      Where can I flee from your
        presence?
If I go up to the heavens, you
      are there;
      if I make my bed in the
        depths, you are there.
If I rise on the wings of the
      dawn,
      if I settle on the far side of
        the sea,
even there your hand will guide
      me,
      your right hand will hold me
        fast.
           PSALM 139:7–10

When loneliness overtakes us, we need to
remember that we are not alone. God has
promised to be with us. He will never forsake
us. Lean on his promises and receive his peace.

Why are you downcast, O my
      soul?
      Why so disturbed within me?
Put your hope in God,
      for I will yet praise him,
      my Savior and my God.
           PSALM 42:11

"I will be with you; I will never leave you nor
forsake you," [says the LORD.]
         JOSHUA 1:5

Who shall separate us from the love of Christ?
Shall trouble or hardship or persecution or
famine or nakedness or danger or sword?...
No, in all these things we are more than conquerors through him who loved us. For I am
convinced that neither death nor life, neither
angels nor demons, neither the present nor
the future, nor any powers, neither height nor
depth, nor anything else in all creation, will
be able to separate us from the love of God
that is in Christ Jesus our Lord.

ROMANS 8:35-39

GOD IS WITH US...

In Our Sorrow

I realized that this was at the lowest and saddest times of my life.

*S*orrow can cause us to doubt God's plan. The psalmist cried, "Has his unfailing love vanished forever? Has his promise failed for all time? Has God forgotten to be merciful? Has he in anger withheld his compassion?" (Psalm 77:8–9). Though we may face trouble and difficulties, sadness and pain, God is still in control, and he is always with us.

> When I said, "My foot is
> slipping,"
> your love, O LORD, supported
> me.
> When anxiety was great within
> me,
> your consolation brought joy
> to my soul.
>> PSALM 94:18–19

> The LORD upholds all those
> who fall
> and lifts up all who are
> bowed down.
>> PSALM 145:14

> The LORD is a refuge for the
> oppressed,
> a stronghold in times of
> trouble.
>> PSALM 9:9

The eternal God is your
refuge,
and underneath are the
everlasting arms.
DEUTERONOMY 33:27

We must remember to listen closely to God's voice when trouble rages around us. When the agonies of life begin to crush us, God has not moved away from us. Often we have moved away from him. We need to return to him in faith and call on him for his strength.

I have put my trust in
you.
Show me the way I should
go,
for to you I lift up my
soul.
PSALM 143:8

The LORD…makes his steps firm;
though he stumble, he will not
fall,
for the LORD upholds him
with his hand.
PSALM 37:23–24

I sought the LORD, and he
answered me;
he delivered me from all my
fears.
PSALM 34:4

*A righteous man may have
     many troubles,
   but the LORD delivers him
     from them all.*

PSALM 34:19

*My soul finds rest in God
     alone;
   my salvation comes from
     him.
He alone is my rock and my
     salvation;
   he is my fortress, I will never
     be shaken.*

PSALM 62:1–2

Do not let your hearts be troubled. Trust in God.

JOHN 14:1

[Jesus said,] "Peace I leave with you; my peace I give you. I do not give to you as the world gives. Do not let your hearts be troubled and do not be afraid."

JOHN 14:27

[Jesus told his disciples,] "In this world you will have trouble. But take heart! I have overcome the world."

JOHN 16:33

[Jesus] said to me, "My grace is sufficient for you, for my power is made perfect in weakness."

2 CORINTHIANS 12:9

Praise be to the God and Father of our Lord
Jesus Christ, the Father of compassion and
the God of all comfort, who comforts us in
all our troubles, so that we can comfort those
in any trouble with the comfort we ourselves
have received from God.

2 CORINTHIANS 1:3–4

The LORD has
anointed me...
to comfort all who mourn...
and...to bestow on them a crown of
beauty
instead of ashes,
the oil of gladness
instead of mourning,
and a garment of praise
instead of a spirit of despair.

ISAIAH 61:1–3

My comfort in my suffering is
this:
Your promise preserves my
life, [O LORD.]

PSALM 119:50

We do not have a high priest who is unable to
sympathize with our weaknesses....Let us
then approach the throne of grace with confidence, so that we may receive mercy and
find grace to help us in our time of need.

HEBREWS 4:15–16

*J*esus experienced sorrow of the deepest kind in the Garden of Gethsemane—the sorrow of impending death. We also experience pain when death takes a loved one, but God reminds us that he is still in control. Death is not the master—God is.

> For none of us lives to himself alone and none of us dies to himself alone. If we live, we live to the Lord; and if we die, we die to the Lord. So, whether we live or die, we belong to the Lord.
>
> ROMANS 14:7–8

> If only for this life we have hope in Christ, we are to be pitied more than all men. But Christ has indeed been raised from the dead...
> Since death came through a man, the resurrection of the dead comes also through a man. For as in Adam all die, so in Christ all will be made alive.
>
> 1 CORINTHIANS 15:19–22

> Listen, I tell you a mystery: We will not all sleep, but we will all be changed—in a flash, in the twinkling of an eye, at the last trumpet. For the trumpet will sound, the dead will be raised imperishable, and we will be changed.
>
> 1 CORINTHIANS 15:51–52

Even though I walk
through the valley of the
shadow of death,
I will fear no evil,
for you are with me;
your rod and your staff,
they comfort me.

PSALM 23:4

We believe that…God will bring with Jesus those who have fallen asleep in him…For the Lord himself will come down from heaven, with a loud command, with the voice of the archangel and with the trumpet call of God, and the dead in Christ will rise first. After that, we who are still alive and are left will be caught up together with them in the clouds to meet the Lord in the air. And so we will be with the Lord forever.

1 THESSALONIANS 4:14,16-17

For to me, to live is Christ and to die is gain.

PHILIPPIANS 1:21

Whether we face death, discouragement, loss, or pain, we can take great comfort in knowing that no sorrow is too deep that God cannot feel it with us. And God wants to help deliver us from it. He wants to bring us his divine comfort.

This I call to mind
*   and therefore I have hope:*
Because of the LORD's great
*   love we are not*
*   consumed,*
*   for his compassions never*
*   fail.*
They are new every morning;
*   great is your faithfulness.*
            LAMENTATIONS 3:21–23

The LORD is good to those
*   whose hope is in him,*
*   to the one who seeks him.*
            LAMENTATIONS 3:25

Do not be anxious about anything, but in everything, by prayer and petition, with thanksgiving, present your requests to God. And the peace of God, which transcends all understanding, will guard your hearts and your minds in Christ Jesus.
            PHILIPPIANS 4:6–7

Be strong and take heart,
*   all you who hope in the LORD.*
            PSALM 31:24

[God] will show compassion,
so great is his unfailing
love.
LAMENTATIONS 3:32

[Jesus said,] "Come to me, all you who are
weary and burdened, and I will give you rest.
Take my yoke upon you and learn from me,
for I am gentle and humble in heart, and you
will find rest for your souls."
MATTHEW 11:28–29

"I will refresh the weary and satisfy the faint,"
[says the LORD.]
JEREMIAH 31:25

For I am the LORD, your God,
who takes hold of your right
hand
and says to you, Do not fear;
I will help you.
ISAIAH 41:13

In all their distress [the LORD] too was
distressed,
and the angel of his
presence saved them.
In his love and mercy he
redeemed them;
he lifted them up and
carried them.
ISAIAH 63:9

Shout for joy, O heavens;
rejoice, O earth;
burst into song,
O mountains!
For the LORD comforts his
people
and will have compassion on
his afflicted ones.

ISAIAH 49:13

I will build them up and not tear them down;
I will plant them and not uproot them. I will
give them a heart to know me, that I am the
LORD. They will be my people, and I will be
their God.

JEREMIAH 24:6–7

*T*hough things may seem hopeless, "God, who
has called you into fellowship with his Son
Jesus Christ our Lord, is faithful" (1 Corinthians
1:9). No trial is so great that God cannot deliver
us. No pain is so great that he does not bring us
comfort. And no situation is ever without God's
presence: "Do not fear, for I am with you; do
not be dismayed, for I am your God. I will
strengthen you and help you; I will uphold you
with my righteous right hand" (Isaiah 41:10).

GOD IS WITH US...

Should We Fret?

This always bothered me...

Fretting and a kitchen blender have a lot in common. With the push of a button, the contents of a blender are whirled and swirled until they become a frothy mixture. In our lives, fretting gnaws away at us until our lives become a churned jumble. But God doesn't want us to live "blender-ized" lives.

> Do not fret because of evil
>   men
>   or be envious of those who
>   do wrong;
> for like the grass they will soon
>   wither,
>   like green plants they will
>   soon die away.
> Trust in the LORD and do good.
>   PSALM 37:1–3

Fretting easily leads to worry; worry casts a big shadow over small problems—a shadow that should never cross our lives.

> Cast all your anxiety on [God] because he cares for you.
>   1 PETER 5:7

> Jesus said…"Do not worry about your life, what you will eat; or about your body, what you will wear. Life is more than food, and the body more than clothes."
>   LUKE 12:22–23

Who of you by worrying can add a single hour to his life? And why do you worry about clothes? See how the lilies of the field grow. They do not labor or spin. Yet I tell you that not even Solomon in all his splendor was dressed like one of these. If that is how God clothes the grass of the field, which is here today and tomorrow is thrown into the fire, will he not much more clothe you, O you of little faith?

MATTHEW 6:27–30

When the outlook is not good, we should not fret. We need a change of perspective to realize that God sees tomorrow more clearly than we see yesterday. The future is completely in his hands!

When they heard that the LORD was concerned about them and had seen their misery, they bowed down and worshiped.

EXODUS 4:31

"I am concerned for you and will look on you with favor," [says the LORD.]

EZEKIEL 36:9

Don't fret! Cheer up! Neither the sun, nor the Son, have gone out of business. He is with us. A new day will dawn, and the Lord will bring himself to the center of our problems.

> *Blessed is the man who*
> *   trusts in the LORD,*
> *   whose confidence is in him.*
> *He will be like a tree planted*
> *   by the water*
> *   that sends out its roots by*
> *   the stream.*
> *It does not fear when heat*
> *   comes;*
> *   its leaves are always green.*
> *It has no worries in a year of*
> *   drought*
> *   and never fails to bear*
> *   fruit.*
>
> JEREMIAH 17:7–8

> *Cast your cares on the LORD*
> *   and he will sustain you;*
> *   he will never let the*
> *   righteous fall.*
>
> PSALM 55:22

Let us then approach the throne of grace with confidence, so that we may receive mercy and find grace to help us in our time of need.

HEBREWS 4:16

The LORD is with you when you are with him. If you seek him, he will be found by you.

2 CHRONICLES 15:2

My flesh and my heart may
*   fail,*
*   but God is the strength of my*
*   heart*
*   and my portion forever.*
PSALM 73:26

Be on your guard; stand firm in the faith; be men of courage; be strong.
1 CORINTHIANS 16:13

He who fears the LORD has a
*   secure fortress.*
PROVERBS 14:26

Great peace have they who
*   love [God's] law,*
*   and nothing can make them*
*   stumble.*
PSALM 119:165

God has said, "Never will I leave you; never will I forsake you." So we say with confidence, "The Lord is my helper; I will not be afraid. What can man do to me?"
HEBREWS 13:5–6

The LORD himself goes before you and will be with you; he will never leave you nor forsake you. Do not be afraid; do not be discouraged.
DEUTERONOMY 31:8

*R*emember, fretting will only tie us in knots. Prayer is the only way to cut short our fretting—to untie those knots of worry and care and grant us God's peace, instead.

> Do not be anxious about anything, but in everything, by prayer and petition, with thanksgiving, present your requests to God. And the peace of God, which transcends all understanding, will guard your hearts and your minds in Christ Jesus.
>
> PHILIPPIANS 4:6—7

GOD IS WITH US...

When We Need Direction

*And I questioned the Lord
about my dilemma.*

When a transit strike brought our recently purchased business to a standstill, I found myself wondering if we had made the right decision to get into this new business. The choice had seemed to be the right one at the time, but then, I wasn't so sure. How was I supposed to sort out what we should do next? When we face questions of this kind, we need to get our arms around God's wisdom ...

> If any of you lacks wisdom, he should ask God, who gives generously to all without finding fault, and it will be given to him.
>
> JAMES 1:5

> *"I will instruct you and teach*
> *you in the way you*
> *should go;*
> *I will counsel you and watch*
> *over you," [says the LORD.]*
>
> PSALM 32:8

> *Trust in the LORD with all*
> *your heart*
> *and lean not on your own*
> *understanding;*
> *in all your ways acknowledge*
> *him,*
> *and he will make your*
> *paths straight.*
>
> PROVERBS 3:5–6

For the LORD gives wisdom,
*   and from his mouth come*
*   knowledge and*
*   understanding.*
              PROVERBS 2:6

Whether you turn to the right or to the left,
your ears will hear a voice behind you, saying,
"This is the way; walk in it."
              ISAIAH 30:21

But when he, the Spirit of truth, comes, he
will guide you into all truth. He will not
speak on his own; he will speak only what he
hears, and he will tell you what is yet to come.
              JOHN 16:13

Show me your ways, O LORD,
*   teach me your paths;*
guide me in your truth and
*   teach me,*
*   for you are God my Savior,*
*   and my hope is in you all day*
*   long.*
              PSALM 25:4–5

This is what the LORD says—
*   your Redeemer, the Holy*
*   One of Israel:*
"I am the LORD your God,
*   who teaches you what is best*
*   for you,*
*   who directs you in the*
*   way you should go."*
              ISAIAH 48:17

God doesn't mind our questions when we come to him with a seeking heart. God is bigger than any question we can ask. And he often will give us the answers we seek in his Word.

> Your word is a lamp to my
>   feet
> and a light for my path.
>
> PSALM 119:105

> These commands are a
>   lamp,
>   this teaching is a light,
> and the corrections of
>   discipline
>   are the way to life.
>
> PROVERBS 6:23

Do not let this Book of the Law depart from your mouth; meditate on it day and night, so that you may be careful to do everything written in it. Then you will be prosperous and successful.

JOSHUA 1:8

> Pay attention and listen to the
>   sayings of the wise…
> for it is pleasing when you keep
>   them in your heart
>   and have all of them ready
>   on your lips.
> So that your trust may be in
>   the LORD.
>
> PROVERBS 22:17−19

When we find ourselves questioning God's reason for allowing certain things to happen, we must stop, remember God's faithfulness, and depend upon his grace. Whatever our questions, whatever our circumstances, God is still in control.

> If the LORD delights in a
>   man's way,
>   he makes his steps firm;
> though he stumble, he will not
>   fall,
>   for the LORD upholds him
>   with his hand.
>   PSALM 37:23—24

> Since you are my rock and my
>   fortress,
>   for the sake of your name
>   lead and guide me, [O LORD.]
>   PSALM 31:3

And we know that in all things God works for the good of those who love him, who have been called according to his purpose.
          ROMANS 8:28

> The LORD will fulfill his purpose
>   for me;
>   your love, O LORD, endures
>   forever—
> do not abandon the works of
>   your hands.
>   PSALM 138:8

Let us acknowledge the LORD;
let us press on to
acknowledge him.
As surely as the sun rises,
he will appear;
he will come to us like the
winter rains,
like the spring rains that
water the earth.

HOSEA 6:3

For this God is our God for
ever and ever;
he will be our guide even to
the end.

PSALM 48:14

When we need direction, we must trust that
the Lord will take our faith, limited as it is,
and make something of lasting value out of it.
God has a plan for us. He cares about our
dilemmas, hears our heartfelt cries, and will
answer us in ways that will astonish us and fill
our hearts with songs of joy.

"For I know the plans I have for you,"
declares the LORD, "plans to prosper you and
not to harm you, plans to give you hope and
a future."

JEREMIAH 29:11

GOD IS WITH US...
In Our Decisions

"Lord, You told me when I decided to follow You..."

It seems that sometimes all we do is make decisions. Purchases at the grocery store are easy, but life-changing decisions are more difficult. How can God help us?

> [The Lord says,] "I guide you in the way of
>   wisdom
>   and lead you along straight
>   paths."
>   PROVERBS 4:11

> The Lord gives wisdom,
>   and from his mouth come
>   knowledge and
>   understanding.
>   PROVERBS 2:6

> Do you not know?
>   Have you not heard?
> The Lord is the everlasting
>   God,
>   the Creator of the ends of
>   the earth.
> He will not grow tired or weary,
>   and his understanding no
>   one can fathom.
> He gives strength to the weary
>   and increases the power of
>   the weak.
>   ISAIAH 40:28-29

Where then does wisdom
come from?
Where does understanding
dwell?
It is hidden from the eyes of
every living thing,
concealed even from the
birds of the air...
God understands the way to it
and he alone knows where it
dwells.

JOB 28:20—21, 23

If any of you lacks wisdom, he should ask God, who gives generously to all without finding fault, and it will be given to him.

JAMES 1:5

*T*he decisions we need to make may be simple or they may be complex, but they should always be predicated on our decision to follow the Lord.

What does the LORD your God ask of you but to fear the LORD your God, to walk in all his ways, to love him, to serve the LORD your God with all your heart and with all your soul, and to observe the LORD's commands and decrees that I am giving you today for your own good?

DEUTERONOMY 10:12—13

Fear the LORD and serve him faithfully with all your heart; consider what great things he has done for you.

1 SAMUEL 12:24

[Jesus said,] "Whoever acknowledges me before men, I will also acknowledge him before my Father in heaven."

MATTHEW 10:32

[Joshua said,] "Choose for yourselves this day whom you will serve...As for me and my household, we will serve the LORD."

JOSHUA 24:15

Love the LORD your God, to walk in all his ways, to obey his commands, to hold fast to him and to serve him with all your heart and all your soul.

JOSHUA 22:5

It is the LORD your God you must follow, and him you must revere. Keep his commands and obey him; serve him and hold fast to him.

DEUTERONOMY 13:4

When we decide to follow the Lord, it means we must live our lives the way he wants us to, following his commands, yielding to his control.

> Those who live according to the sinful nature have their minds set on what that nature desires; but those who live in accordance with the Spirit have their minds set on what the Spirit desires.
>
> ROMANS 8:5

> The one who sows to please his sinful nature, from that nature will reap destruction; the one who sows to please the Spirit, from the Spirit will reap eternal life.
>
> GALATIANS 6:8

> Forgetting what is behind and straining toward what is ahead, I press on toward the goal to win the prize for which God has called me heavenward in Christ Jesus.
>
> PHILIPPIANS 3:13–14

The grace of God that brings salvation has appeared to all men. It teaches us to say "No" to ungodliness and worldly passions, and to live self-controlled, upright and godly lives in this present age.

TITUS 2:11–12

Make every effort to live in peace with all men and to be holy.

HEBREWS 12:14

Offer your bodies as living sacrifices, holy and pleasing to God—this is your spiritual act of worship. Do not conform any longer to the pattern of this world, but be transformed by the renewing of your mind.

ROMANS 12:1–2

God did not call us to be impure, but to live a holy life.

1 THESSALONIANS 4:7

What does the LORD your God ask of you but to fear the LORD your God, to walk in all his ways, to love him, to serve the LORD your God with all your heart and with all your soul?

DEUTERONOMY 10:12

Pursue righteousness, godliness, faith, love, endurance and gentleness. Fight the good fight of the faith.

1 TIMOTHY 6:11–12

Serve him with wholehearted devotion and with a willing mind, for the LORD searches every heart and understands every motive behind the thoughts.

1 CHRONICLES 28:9

"Obey me, and I will be your God and you will be my people. Walk in all the ways I command you, that it may go well with you," [says the LORD Almighty.]

JEREMIAH 7:23

Now that you have been set free from sin and have become slaves to God, the benefit you reap leads to holiness, and the result is eternal life.

ROMANS 6:22

Let us purify ourselves from everything that contaminates body and spirit, perfecting holiness out of reverence for God.

2 CORINTHIANS 7:1

Be holy in all you do; for it is written: "Be holy, because I am holy."

1 PETER 1:15—16

Just as you received Christ Jesus as Lord, continue to live in him, rooted and built up in him, strengthened in the faith as you were taught, and overflowing with thankfulness.

COLOSSIANS 2:6—7

Do not turn away from the LORD, but serve the LORD with all your heart.

1 SAMUEL 12:20

Let your eyes look straight
ahead,
fix your gaze directly before
you.
Make level paths for your
feet
and take only ways that are
firm.

PROVERBS 4:25—26

We must pay more careful attention, therefore, to what we have heard, so that we do not drift away.

HEBREWS 2:1

Let us hold unswervingly to the hope we profess, for he who promised is faithful.

HEBREWS 10:23

Since we are surrounded by such a great cloud of witnesses, let us throw off everything that hinders and the sin that so easily entangles, and let us run with perseverance the race marked out for us.

HEBREWS 12:1

This is how we know who the children of God are and who the children of the devil are: Anyone who does not do what is right is not a child of God; nor is anyone who does not love his brother.

1 JOHN 3:10

He follows my decrees
and faithfully keeps my laws.
That man is righteous;
he will surely live,
declares the Sovereign
LORD.

EZEKIEL 18:9

He has showed you, O man,
what is good.
And what does the LORD
require of you?
To act justly and to love
mercy
and to walk humbly with
your God.

MICAH 6:8

LORD, who may dwell in your
sanctuary?
Who may live on your holy
hill?
He whose walk is blameless
and who does what is
righteous,
who speaks the truth from his
heart.

PSALM 15:1—2

We all need God's divine power from day to day to follow in his footsteps—to learn the eternal, upside-down, inside-out values of God's kingdom so that we may make decisions based on his character and ultimately share in his glory.

> If anyone speaks, he should do it as one speaking the very words of God. If anyone serves, he should do it with the strength God provides, so that in all things God may be praised through Jesus Christ.
>
> 1 PETER 4:11

GOD IS WITH US...
As Our Guide

"...You would walk and talk
with me all the way."

I saw two children walking together today, happily exchanging words and glances, laughing aloud at shared jokes. They didn't worry about the cracks in the sidewalk or the bumps in the road but, rather, skipped along over them. God wants our walk with him to be just like that— enjoying his company, sharing together, and crossing the rough places on our journey home without the slightest care.

> If we claim to have fellowship with him yet walk in the darkness, we lie and do not live by the truth. But if we walk in the light, as he is in the light, we have fellowship with one another, and the blood of Jesus, his Son, purifies us from all sin.
>
> 1 JOHN 1:6–7

> Whoever claims to live in him must walk as Jesus did.
>
> 1 JOHN 2:6

> *Righteousness goes before him*
> *and prepares the way for his*
> *steps.*
>
> PSALM 85:13

> O LORD...I have walked before you faithfully and with wholehearted devotion and have done what is good in your eyes.
>
> 2 KINGS 20:3

You have delivered me
from death
and my feet from stumbling,
that I may walk before God
in the light of life.

PSALM 56:13

Blessed are those who have
learned to acclaim you,
who walk in the light of
your presence, O LORD.

PSALM 89:15

The ways of the LORD are
right;
the righteous walk in them,
but the rebellious stumble in
them.

HOSEA 14:9

*M*any times along our life-walk, the path
becomes obscure. We need someone to help
show us the way. That someone is God.

The LORD will guide you always;
he will satisfy your needs in
a sun-scorched land
and will strengthen your
frame.
You will be like a well-watered
garden,
like a spring whose waters
never fail.

ISAIAH 58:11

[God] guides me in paths of
    righteousness
    for his name's sake.
Even though I walk
    through the valley of the
        shadow of death,
I will fear no evil,
    for you are with me;
your rod and your staff,
    they comfort me.

PSALM 23:3–4

This is what the LORD says—
    your Redeemer, the Holy
        One of Israel:
"I am the LORD your God,
    who teaches you what is best
        for you,
    who directs you in the
        way you should go."

ISAIAH 48:17

[O LORD,] you guide me with your
    counsel.

PSALM 73:24

When he, the Spirit of truth, comes, he will
guide you into all truth.

JOHN 16:13

[O LORD,] since you are my rock and my
    fortress,
    for the sake of your name
        lead and guide me.

PSALM 31:3

If any of you lacks wisdom, he should ask God, who gives generously to all without finding fault, and it will be given to him.

JAMES 1:5

Teach me your way, O LORD;
lead me in a straight path.

PSALM 27:11

Trust in the LORD with all
your heart
and lean not on your own
understanding;
in all your ways acknowledge
him,
and he will make your
paths straight.

PROVERBS 3:5—6

Lead me, O LORD, in your
righteousness...
make straight your way
before me.

PSALM 5:8

Show me the way I should
go,
for to you I lift up my
soul.

PSALM 143:8

Teach me to do your will,
for you are my God;
may your good Spirit
lead me on level ground.

PSALM 143:10

87

$\mathcal{G}$od's Word becomes the road map for our daily walk with the Savior.

> Your word is a lamp to my
>   feet
>   and a light for my path, O LORD.
>
> PSALM 119:105

> These commands are a
>   lamp,
>   this teaching is a light,
> and the corrections of
>   discipline
>   are the way to life.
>
> PROVERBS 6:23

$\mathcal{H}$is Word reminds us of his power, his provision, and his sovereignty.

> Commit to the LORD whatever
>   you do,
>   and your plans will
>   succeed.
>
> PROVERBS 16:3

> My flesh and my heart may
>   fail,
>   but God is the strength of my
>   heart
>   and my portion forever.
>
> PSALM 73:26

If the LORD delights in a
*   man's way,*
* he makes his steps firm;*
though he stumble, he will not
*   fall,*
*   for the LORD upholds him*
*   with his hand.*

PSALM 37:23–24

*H*is Word reminds us of his love.

This I call to mind
*   and therefore I have hope:*
Because of the LORD's great
*   love we are not*
*   consumed,*
*   for his compassions never*
*   fail.*
They are new every morning;
*   great is your faithfulness.*

LAMENTATIONS 3:21–23

The LORD will fulfill [his purpose]
*   for me;*
* your love, O LORD, endures*
*   forever.*

PSALM 138:8

How great is the love the Father has lavished
on us, that we should be called children of
God!

1 JOHN 3:1

*L*et's enjoy the time with God as he walks and talks with us each day, wherever we are, for "this God is our God for ever and ever; he will be our guide even to the end" (Psalm 48:14).

> *"Be still, and know that I am*
> *God;*
> *I will be exalted among the*
> *nations,*
> *I will be exalted in the*
> *earth."*
> *The* LORD *Almighty is with us;*
> *the God of Jacob is our*
> *fortress.*
> PSALM 46:10—11

GOD IS WITH US...

In Our Difficulties

But I'm aware that during the most troublesome times of my life, there is only one set of footprints.

Ruts and potholes. Shadows and deep darkness. The journey of life can sometimes be very troubling. We stumble and have difficulty following in God's footsteps. We are fearful of the unknown. But God's Word reminds us to trust, to believe, to hope.

> Blessed is he whose help is
>   the God of Jacob,
>   whose hope is in the LORD his
>   God,
> the Maker of heaven and
>   earth,
>   the sea, and everything in
>   them—
>   the LORD, who remains
>   faithful forever.
>
> PSALM 146:5–6

> Why are you downcast, O my
>   soul?
>   Why so disturbed within me?
> Put your hope in God,
>   for I will yet praise him,
>   my Savior and my God.
>
> PSALM 43:5–6

> You have been my hope,
>   O Sovereign LORD,
>   my confidence since my
>   youth.
>
> PSALM 71:5

Blessed is the man who
trusts in the LORD,
whose confidence is in him.

JEREMIAH 17:7

The LORD is good to those
whose hope is in him,
to the one who seeks him.

LAMENTATIONS 3:25

When I am afraid,
I will trust in you.
In God, whose word I praise,
in God I trust; I will not be
afraid.
What can mortal man do to
me?

PSALM 56:3—4

As for me, I watch in
hope for the LORD,
I wait for God my Savior;
my God will hear me.

MICAH 7:7

We all go through troubling times, but we must never doubt God's presence with us.

God has said, "Never will I leave you; never will I forsake you." So we say with confidence, "The Lord is my helper; I will not be afraid. What can man do to me?"

HEBREWS 13:5–6

[Jesus said,] "Surely I am with you always, to the very end of the age."

MATTHEW 28:20

Do not fear, for I am with
*   you;*
*   do not be dismayed, for I am*
*   your God.*
I will strengthen you and help
*   you;*
*   I will uphold you with my*
*   righteous right hand.*

ISAIAH 41:10

The LORD your God is a merciful God; he will not abandon or destroy you.

DEUTERONOMY 4:31

Those who know your name
*   will trust in you,*
*   for you, LORD, have never*
*   forsaken those who*
*   seek you.*

PSALM 9:10

"For I know the plans I have for you," declares the LORD, "plans to prosper you and not to harm you, plans to give you hope and a future."

JEREMIAH 29:11

God will never let us down. He promises us his strength, his peace, his comfort, and his presence. All we need to do is depend on him, for we can never break God's promises by leaning on them.

> Do not be afraid. Stand firm and you will see the deliverance the LORD will bring you today.... The LORD will fight for you; you need only to be still.
>
> EXODUS 14:13–14

> *The eternal God is your*
> *refuge,*
> *and underneath are the*
> *everlasting arms.*
>
> DEUTERONOMY 33:27

> "I will build them up and not tear them down; I will plant them and not uproot them. I will give them a heart to know me, that I am the LORD. They will be my people, and I will be their God, for they will return to me with all their heart," [says the LORD.]
>
> JEREMIAH 24:6–7

> *The LORD longs to be*
> *gracious to you;*
> *he rises to show you*
> *compassion.*
>
> ISAIAH 30:18

[Jesus replied,] "In this world you will have trouble. But take heart! I have overcome the world."

JOHN 16:33

We know that in all things God works for the good of those who love him, who have been called according to his purpose.

ROMANS 8:28

If the LORD delights in a
        man's way,
    he makes his steps firm;
though he stumble, he will not
        fall,
    for the LORD upholds him
        with his hand.

PSALM 37:23—24

"Call upon me in the day
        of trouble;
    I will deliver you, and you
        will honor me," [says the LORD.]

PSALM 50:15

Cast your cares on the LORD
    and he will sustain you;
    he will never let the
        righteous fall.

PSALM 55:22

He gives strength to the weary
    and increases the power of
      the weak.
Even youths grow tired and
      weary,
    and young men stumble
      and fall;
but those who hope in the
      LORD
    will renew their strength.
They will soar on wings like
      eagles;
    they will run and not grow
      weary,
    they will walk and not be
      faint.

ISAIAH 40:29−31

"When you pass through the
      waters,
    I will be with you;
and when you pass through the
      rivers,
    they will not sweep over you.
When you walk through the
      fire,
    you will not be burned;
    the flames will not set you
      ablaze," [says the LORD.*]*

ISAIAH 43:2

The LORD *is good,*
    a refuge in times of trouble.
He cares for those who trust
    in him.

NAHUM 1:7

Who shall separate us from the love of
Christ? Shall trouble or hardship or persecution or famine or nakedness or danger or
sword....No, in all these things we are more
than conquerors through him who loved us.

ROMANS 8:35,37

*T*hose things we consider difficulties are often
God's opportunities for our greater blessing.
We must trust, believe, hope, and continue to
walk the path he has laid before us.

May our Lord Jesus Christ himself and God
our Father, who loved us and by his grace gave
us eternal encouragement and good hope,
encourage your hearts and strengthen you in
every good deed and word.

2 THESSALONIANS 2:16—17

GOD IS WITH US...

In Our Confusion

*I just don't understand
why, when I needed You
most, You leave me.*

*M*any things in life cannot be explained: the death of an infant, the loss of a job, the rebellion of a child, the desertion by a loved one, or any number of other circumstances beyond our control. Have you ever wondered, *Why did this have to happen?* God can help us with those "Why?" questions.

[David questioned God,]
"Has his unfailing love vanished
forever?
Has his promise failed for
all time?
Has God forgotten to be
merciful?
Has he in anger withheld his
compassion?"

PSALM 77:8–9

"My thoughts are not your
thoughts,
neither are your ways my
ways,"
declares the LORD.
"As the heavens are higher
than the earth,
so are my ways higher than
your ways
and my thoughts than your
thoughts."

ISAIAH 55:8–9

When faced with bewildering circumstances, we are tempted to ask "Why?" But a better question to ask is "What?…What do you have in mind now, Lord?"

"Call to me and I will answer you and tell you great and unsearchable things you do not know," [says the LORD.]

JEREMIAH 33:3

Cast your cares on the LORD
*   and he will sustain you;*
*   he will never let the*
*   righteous fall.*

PSALM 55:22

Let us acknowledge the LORD;
*   let us press on to*
*   acknowledge him.*
As surely as the sun rises,
*   he will appear;*
he will come to us like the
*   winter rains,*
*   like the spring rains that*
*   water the earth.*

HOSEA 6:3

[O LORD,] it was good for me to be
*   afflicted*
*   so that I might learn your*
*   decrees.*

PSALM 119:71

Though it may sometimes seem that things are out of control, we can take comfort in God's enduring promises and constant presence.

[The LORD says,] "Do not fear, for I am with
        you;
    do not be dismayed, for I am
        your God.
I will strengthen you and help
        you;
    I will uphold you with my
        righteous right hand."
            ISAIAH 41:10

A righteous man may have
        many troubles,
    but the LORD delivers him
        from them all.
            PSALM 34:19

"I will make an everlasting covenant with them: I will never stop doing good to them," [says the LORD.]
            JEREMIAH 32:40

Your love, O LORD, endures
        forever.
            PSALM 138:8

Be strong and courageous. Do not be terrified; do not be discouraged, for the LORD your God will be with you wherever you go.
            JOSHUA 1:9

Let us hold unswervingly to the hope we profess, for [God] who promised is faithful.

HEBREWS 10:23

God, who has called you into fellowship with
his Son Jesus Christ our Lord, is faithful.

1 CORINTHIANS 1:9

Who is a God like you,
*   who pardons sin and*
*   forgives the*
*   transgression*
*   of the remnant of his*
*   inheritance?*
You do not stay angry forever
*   but delight to show mercy.*
You will again have compassion
*   on us.*

MICAH 7:18—19

His mercy extends to those who fear him,
*   from generation to generation.*

LUKE 1:50

This I call to mind
*   and therefore I have hope:*
Because of the LORD's great
*   love we are not*
*   consumed,*
*   for his compassions never*
*   fail.*
They are new every morning;
*   great is your faithfulness.*

LAMENTATIONS 3:21—23

Commit to the LORD whatever
you do,
and your plans will
succeed.

PROVERBS 16:3

The LORD is good to those
whose hope is in him,
to the one who seeks him.

LAMENTATIONS 3:25

[O LORD,] you are my hiding place;
you will protect me from
trouble
and surround me with songs
of deliverance.

PSALM 32:7

Blessed are you who hunger now, for you will be satisfied. Blessed are you who weep now, for you will laugh.

LUKE 6:21

*P*ut away all doubts. Cast out all confusion. Stand firm in the work of the Lord, and find a renewed faith following in his footsteps.

The LORD is my strength and
my shield;
my heart trusts in him, and
I am helped.
My heart leaps for joy
and I will give thanks to him.

PSALM 28:7

GOD IS WITH US...

As Our Loving Father

He whispered, "My precious child..."

The Creator of the universe calls me his child—what a blessing! What a privilege! What a responsibility!

> The LORD disciplines
>   those he loves,
>   as a father the son he
>   delights in.
>
> PROVERBS 3:12

> "I will be a Father to you,
>   and you will be my sons and daughters, says the
> Lord Almighty."
>
> 2 CORINTHIANS 6:18

Endure hardship as discipline; God is treating you as sons. For what son is not disciplined by his father?

> HEBREWS 12:7

[David declared,] "You are
    my Father,
  my God, the Rock my
    Savior."

> PSALM 89:26

> To us a child is born,
>   to us a son is given,
>   and the government will be
>   on his shoulders.
> And he will be called...
>   Everlasting Father.
>
> ISAIAH 9:6

O LORD, you are our
*   Father.*
* We are the clay, you are the*
*   potter;*
* we are all the work of your*
*   hand.*
               ISAIAH 64:8

You did not receive a spirit that makes you a slave again to fear, but you received the Spirit of sonship. And by him we cry, "Abba, Father."
               ROMANS 8:15

For us there is but one God, the Father, from whom all things came and for whom we live; and there is but one Lord, Jesus Christ, through whom all things came and through whom we live.
               1 CORINTHIANS 8:6

There is one body and one Spirit—just as you were called to one hope when you were called—one Lord, one faith, one baptism; one God and Father of all, who is over all and through all and in all.
               EPHESIANS 4:4–6

How great is the love the Father has lavished on us, that we should be called children of God!
               1 JOHN 3:1

You, O LORD, are our Father,
* our Redeemer from of old*
*   is your name.*
               ISAIAH 63:16

As children of God we can trust that our Father will provide for us.

> Your Father knows what you need before you ask him.
>
> MATTHEW 6:8

> Which of you fathers, if your son asks for a fish, will give him a snake instead? Or if he asks for an egg, will give him a scorpion? If you then, though you are evil, know how to give good gifts to your children, how much more will your Father in heaven give the Holy Spirit to those who ask him!
>
> LUKE 11:11–13

As God's children, our Father knows us by name and bestows on us certain rights, privileges, and responsibilities.

> *I, the LORD, have called you*
> *in righteousness;*
> *I will take hold of your hand.*
> *I will keep you and will make*
> *you*
> *to be a covenant for the*
> *people*
> *and a light for the Gentiles.*
>
> ISAIAH 42:6

This is what the
      LORD says ...
   he who formed you...
"Fear not, for I have
      redeemed you;
   I have summoned you by
      name; you are mine."
                 ISAIAH 43:1

"I will pour out my Spirit on
      your offspring,
   and my blessing on your
      descendants.
They will spring up like grass in
      a meadow,
   like poplar trees by flowing
      streams.
One will say, 'I belong to the
      LORD';
   another will call himself by
      the name of Jacob;
still another will write on his
   hand, 'The LORD's.' "
               ISAIAH 44:3—5

Before I was born the LORD
      called me;
   from my birth he has made
      mention of my name.
                  ISAIAH 49:1

Our loving Father cares for us as a shepherd cares for his sheep. And we, his children, need to listen carefully to his voice and obey.

The sheep listen to his voice. He calls his own sheep by name and leads them out. When he has brought out all his own, he goes on ahead of them, and his sheep follow him because they know his voice.

JOHN 10:3–4

[Jesus said,] "I am the good shepherd; I know my sheep and my sheep know me—just as the Father knows me and I know the Father—and I lay down my life for the sheep."

JOHN 10:14–15

[Jesus said,] "My sheep listen to my voice; I know them, and they follow me."

JOHN 10:27

GOD IS WITH US...

Always!

*"...I love you and will never
leave you, never, ever, during
your trials and testings."*

We often make promises we can't keep. God isn't like that. God is faithful and trustworthy. When God promises never to leave us, he means just what he says. He's not going anywhere!

God has said, "Never will I leave you; never will I forsake you."

HEBREWS 13:5

The LORD himself goes before you and will be with you; he will never leave you nor forsake you. Do not be afraid; do not be discouraged.

DEUTERONOMY 31:8

"No one will be able to stand up against you all the days of your life. As I was with Moses, so I will be with you; I will never leave you nor forsake you," [says the LORD.]

JOSHUA 1:5

[Jesus replied,] "Surely I am with you always, to the very end of the age."

MATTHEW 28:20

*Do not fear, for I am with
      you;
   do not be dismayed, for I am
      your God.
I will strengthen you and help
      you;
   I will uphold you with my
      righteous right hand.*

ISAIAH 41:10

I am convinced that neither death nor life, neither angels nor demons, neither the present nor the future, nor any powers, neither height nor depth, nor anything else in all creation, will be able to separate us from the love of God that is in Christ Jesus our Lord.

ROMANS 8:38—39

"Though the mountains be
shaken
and the hills be removed,
yet my unfailing love for you
will not be shaken
nor my covenant of peace
be removed,"
says the LORD, *who has*
compassion on you.

ISAIAH 54:10

"Here I am! I stand at the door and knock. If anyone hears my voice and opens the door, I will come in and eat with him, and he with me," [says the Lord.]

REVELATION 3:20

"He will call upon me, and I will
  answer him;
I will be with him in trouble,"
[says the LORD.]

PSALM 91:15

Be strong and courageous. Do not be terrified; do not be discouraged, for the LORD
your God will be with you wherever you go.

JOSHUA 1:9

The LORD watches over you—
  the LORD is your shade at
    your right hand;
the sun will not harm you by
    day,
  nor the moon by night.
The LORD will keep you from all
    harm—
  he will watch over your life;
the LORD will watch over your
    coming and going
  both now and forevermore.

PSALM 121:5–8

When it seems that life is whirling out of control, we can take comfort in God's sovereignty and power. He has everything under control. And he will work his will in every circumstance.

> Commit your way to the LORD;
>   trust in him and he will do
>   this:
> He will make your
>   righteousness shine
>   like the dawn,
>   the justice of your cause like
>   the noonday sun.
>   PSALM 37:5—6

> Commit to the LORD whatever
>   you do,
>   and your plans will
>   succeed.
>   PROVERBS 16:3

Do not be anxious about anything, but in everything, by prayer and petition, with thanksgiving, present your requests to God. And the peace of God, which transcends all understanding, will guard your hearts and your minds in Christ Jesus.
           PHILIPPIANS 4:6—7

> Many are the plans in a man's
>   heart,
>   but it is the LORD's purpose
>   that prevails.
>   PROVERBS 19:21

The LORD Almighty has
      purposed, and who can
      thwart him?
His hand is stretched out,
      and who can turn it
      back?

ISAIAH 14:27

"I make known the end from the
      beginning,
    from ancient times, what is
      still to come.
I say: My purpose will stand,
    and I will do all that I please," [says the LORD.]

ISAIAH 46:10

Look at the birds of the air; they do not sow
or reap or store away in barns, and yet your
heavenly Father feeds them. Are you not
much more valuable than they? Who of you
by worrying can add a single hour to his life?

MATTHEW 6:26–27

I know that you can do all
      things;
    no plan of yours can be
      thwarted, [O LORD.]

JOB 42:2

I know that everything God does will endure
forever; nothing can be added to it and nothing taken from it. God does it so that men
will revere him.

ECCLESIASTES 3:14

The LORD gives strength to his
people;
the LORD blesses his people
with peace.

PSALM 29:11

My flesh and my heart may
fail,
but God is the strength of my
heart
and my portion forever.

PSALM 73:26

[O LORD,] great peace have they who
love your law,
and nothing can make them
stumble.

PSALM 119:165

Those who trust in the LORD are
like Mount Zion,
which cannot be shaken
but endures forever.

PSALM 125:1

Whenever we hit rock-bottom, we can be assured of God's love and care. His encouragement breathes new possibilities into impossible circumstances.

Let us then approach the throne of grace with confidence, so that we may receive mercy and find grace to help us in our time of need.

HEBREWS 4:16

In you, O LORD, I have taken
 refuge;
 let me never be put to
  shame;
 deliver me in your
  righteousness.

PSALM 31:1

The LORD is with me; I will
 not be afraid.

PSALM 118:6

Taste and see that the LORD is
 good;
 blessed is the man who takes
  refuge in him.

PSALM 34:8

So we say with confidence, "The Lord is my helper; I will not be afraid. What can man do to me?"

HEBREWS 13:6

GOD IS WITH US...

As Our Strong Provider

"When you saw only one set of footprints, it was then that I carried you."

*O*ur problems may seem overwhelming, but God's power is stronger than any obstacle we may face.

I am the LORD, the God of all mankind. Is anything too hard for me?
JEREMIAH 32:27

All that we have
accomplished you have
done for us, [O LORD.]
ISAIAH 26:12

[God] does as he pleases
with the powers of heaven
and the peoples of the earth.
No one can hold back his hand
or say to him: "What have
you done?"
DANIEL 4:35

You are the ruler of all
things.
In your hands are strength and
power
to exalt and give strength to
all.
Now, our God, we give you
thanks,
and praise your glorious
name.
1 CHRONICLES 29:12–13

With God all things are possible.
MATTHEW 19:26

The LORD is slow to anger and
great in power....
His way is in the whirlwind and
the storm,
and clouds are the dust of
his feet.
NAHUM 1:3

I can do everything through Christ who gives
me strength.
PHILIPPIANS 4:13

Be strong in the Lord and in his mighty
power.
EPHESIANS 6:10

The eternal God is your
refuge,
and underneath are the
everlasting arms.
DEUTERONOMY 33:27

The LORD gives strength to his
people;
the LORD blesses his people
with peace.
PSALM 29:11

[The Lord] said to me, "My grace is sufficient
for you, for my power is made perfect in
weakness."
2 CORINTHIANS 12:9

*The LORD is the strength of his
    people,
  a fortress of salvation for his
    anointed one.*

PSALM 28:8

*In the LORD alone
  are righteousness and
    strength.*

ISAIAH 45:24

*"I will strengthen them in the
    LORD
  and in his name they will
    walk,"
      declares the LORD.*

ZECHARIAH 10:12

*"I will refresh the weary and satisfy the faint,"
[says the LORD.]*

JEREMIAH 31:25

*S*ince God is our strong Provider, we can be
assured that he is in control of every aspect of
our lives. He will prepare the way before us. He
will never leave us. And he will provide our
every need.

Those who know your name
will trust in you,
for you, LORD, have never
forsaken those who
seek you.

PSALM 9:10

[Jesus taught his disciples saying,] "If you believe, you will receive whatever you ask for in prayer."

MATTHEW 21:22

No eye has seen,
no ear has heard,
no mind has conceived
what God has prepared for those who love
him.

1 CORINTHIANS 2:9

My God will meet all your needs according to his glorious riches in Christ Jesus.

PHILIPPIANS 4:19

[Jesus said,] "Come to me, all you who are weary and burdened, and I will give you rest."

MATTHEW 11:28

"Before they call I will answer;
while they are still speaking
I will hear," [declares the LORD.]

ISAIAH 65:24

Taste and see that the LORD is
good;
blessed is the man who takes
refuge in him.

PSALM 34:8

O LORD Almighty,
blessed is the man who
trusts in you.

PSALM 84:12

Those who trust in the LORD are
like Mount Zion,
which cannot be shaken
but endures forever.

PSALM 125:1

He who did not spare his own Son, but gave
him up for us all—how will he not also, along
with him, graciously give us all things?

ROMANS 8:32

Praise the LORD, O my soul,
and forget not all his benefits—
who forgives all your sins and heals all your diseases,
who redeems your life from the pit
and crowns you with love and compassion,
who satisfies your desires with good things
so that your youth is renewed like the
eagle's.

PSALM 103:2—5

Praise be to the Lord, to God
our Savior,
who daily bears our
burdens.

PSALM 68:19

You will keep in perfect peace
him whose mind is steadfast,
because he trusts in you, [O LORD.]

ISAIAH 26:3

The LORD longs to be
gracious to you;
he rises to show you
compassion.
For the LORD is a God of
justice.
Blessed are all who wait for
him!

ISAIAH 30:18

Trust in the LORD with all
your heart
and lean not on your own
understanding.

PROVERBS 3:5

He who trusts in the
LORD will prosper.

PROVERBS 28:25

As the Scripture says, "Anyone who trusts in
[Christ] will never be put to shame."

ROMANS 10:11

Our God is strong enough to carry us, but also gentle enough to enfold us in his loving embrace.

[God] tends his flock like a
*   shepherd:*
*   He gathers the lambs in his*
*   arms*
and carries them close to his
*   heart;*
*   he gently leads those that*
*   have young.*

ISAIAH 40:11

[The LORD] makes me lie down in
*   green pastures,*
he leads me beside quiet
*   waters,*
he restores my soul.
He guides me in paths of
*   righteousness*
*   for his name's sake.*

PSALM 23:2-3

[Jesus taught them saying,] "Come to me, all you who are weary and burdened, and I will give you rest. Take my yoke upon you and learn from me, for I am gentle and humble in heart, and you will find rest for your souls. For my yoke is easy and my burden is light."

MATTHEW 11:28-30

As our strong Provider carries us over the rough places in our lives, he speaks words of peace and blessing to our wounded hearts.

> The LORD bless you
>   and keep you;
> the LORD make his face shine
>   upon you
>   and be gracious to you;
> the LORD turn his face toward
>   you
>   and give you peace.
>
> NUMBERS 6:24–26

May the God of peace...equip you with everything good for doing his will, and may he work in us what is pleasing to him, through Jesus Christ, to whom be glory for ever and ever. Amen.

HEBREWS 13:20–21

If you have enjoyed this book,
Hallmark would love
to hear from you.

Please send comments to:

Book Feedback
2501 McGee, Mail Drop 215
Kansas City, MO 64141-6580

Or e-mail us at:

booknotes@hallmark.com